We all belong

Goss
CASTLE

DEDICATION

For everyone

ACKNOWLEDGEMENTS

Illustrator / author: Nathalie Goss
Author / editor: Alex Goss

instagram.com/nathaliegossdesigns

If you look closely, you'll soon see,

no one looks the same as me.

I have lovely dark **curly** hair...

and my hair is straight,

 **long**

and fair.

I am **tall**

I am **small**

We both love
to play football.

I like to be **loud!**

I'm sometimes **shy...**

Who is smart?

You and I

Everyone is different in one way or another.

I even look different to my sister and my brother.

Some might say we're a different race.

We think that's completely

What is our race?

Is it the colour of our skin?

It means we share one kind of thing.

Sharing what?

Sharing looks.

Sharing things in history books.

We're the same in some ways too.

We like

We like

We both like **red**.

We both are kind.

We both like reading

to unwind.

My eyes are **brown**

My eyes are **blue**

When we come together

There's nothing we can't do

It'd be boring if we all looked the same.

If we ate the same food.

If we had the same names.

My family and I eat rice and peas.

That sounds nice, can I try that please?

My family sings precious

My family wears nice

In our school

we  belong...

Together we all get along!

I love my language and the way I speak.

I love my home.

I love my street.

Where I live, the animals squawk.

Near my home, we go for walks.

Not one of us is out of place.

We all belong to the

 Can you draw yourself and a friend?

In what ways are you the same?

In what ways are you different?

You are both **amazing!**

Also available from Goss Castle

Your reviews help us get more kids learning through reading.

Please share your feedback. We read every one!

1. **Go to Amazon**
2. **Click Orders**
3. **Find the book and click** Write a Product Review

Goss
CASTLE

Made in the USA
Middletown, DE
13 November 2021